NIGHT AT MY THROAT

# Night At My Throat

*Poems*

Brian Rihlmann

Pony One Dog Press
Washington, DC

# NIGHT AT MY THROAT

© 2020 Brian Rihlmann

All rights reserved. No part of this book may be reproduced or transmitted in any form or by any means, electronic or mechanical, without written permission from the author, except for the inclusion of brief quotations in a review.

Cover art: *Dervishes* by David Febland
Interior artwork: Alison Chase Radcliffe
Book layout: Barbara Shaw

ISBN 978-0-9753095-9-9

First Edition

Published by:
Pony One Dog Press
Suite 113
1613 Harvard Street, NW
Washington, DC 20009

# Contents

Introduction • xi

## DARK DREAM

    Another Go • 3
    Amen. • 4
    A Younger Version. • 5
    Beyond Pale Suburbia. • 6
    Rattle. • 8
    He's Harmless. • 9
    Surviving Home. • 10

## THE ONE LESS SOUL

    Memories. • 13
    Calling The Wolves. • 14
    A long Life. • 16
    Contrast. • 17
    "Here Comes The Airplane". • 20
    How Do You Want Your Eggs? • 21
    Like It Was. • 23
    One Less Soul. • 24
    Riding The Ride. • 25
    The First Noble Truth Of Wobbly. • 27
    The Whole Point Of The Game. • 29
    Vertigo. • 31
    Michelle. • 32
    Pusillanimous • 33
    Survivor. • 35

## DANCE OF TOUCH

A Box Of Scraps. • 39
Big Questions. • 40
Heart. • 41
Dream Of A Love. • 42
Acceptance. • 43

## THE CLEAR BLUE THAT'S ALWAYS THERE

Making Love Easier. • 47
A Dumb Question. • 49
A Grumpy Guy. • 51
A Solitary Theater. • 53
Anything But This. • 54
Around The Corner. • 55
Be Still, Now. • 56
Bear Trap. • 58
Between Man And Beast. • 59
Break. • 61
Caught In The Groove. • 63
Cobwebs. • 64
Codependency In The Social Media Age. • 65
Coffee Mug. • 67
Conman. • 69
Control Freak. • 71
Conversations. • 73
Deadly. • 74
Drained. • 75
Embarrassment • 77
Eviction. • 78
Except. • 79
Flypaper. • 81

Frozen. • 83
Getting Over, Getting Under. • 84
Heaviness. • 86
Hoarder. • 88
I Die Anyway. • 90
I Smile. • 91
Karma Machines. • 93
Living With This And That. • 95
Loose Ends. • 96
More Than. • 97
My Accomplice. • 99
My Greatest Talent • 101
My Segment. • 103
My Self. • 105
No One Can. • 106
Ode To The Discarded. • 108
On Reductionism. • 109
Over Like A Song. • 110
Peripheral. • 112
Prosthetics. • 113
Rorschach Test. • 114
Scream. • 115
Slowly. • 116
Sobering Up. • 118
So They Say. • 120
Solstice. • 121
Tactics. • 122
Talk About A Mess. • 124
The Juggler And The Alley Cat. • 125
The View From Here. • 128
Told You. • 130
Too Late. • 131

Transference. • 132
Twist Of Grain. • 134
Want. • 136
What We Give. • 138
Whispers. • 139
Wholeness. • 141
The Night At My Throat. • 142

## THE GRASS THAT COVERS US

Fatherhood. • 145
Asking The Question. • 147
How It Might Be. • 149
To Dig, Pace, And Chew. • 150
Understandable. • 151
Stray. • 152

## TWO POEMS

Worms. • 155
Disciple. • 156

## YELLOW BIRD

A Little Longer. • 159
Thank You, Sir. • 160
No Matter What You Say. • 161

*Acknowledgements.* • 164

*About the Author* • 165

## INTRODUCTION

BRIAN RIHLMANN is a poet who has come through the darkness. Those who know him from his first book of poems, Ordinary Trauma, will know how dark that period was. Those poems were the record of the destructive existence of a troubled young man. In this, The Night at My Throat, his latest volume, they'll be heartened to find he has survived, and will read this, his latest work, for both insights and encouragement for their own struggles.

As with Charles Bukowski, an influence and a poet he is sometimes compared to, Rihlmann's America is the dark underside of a life many of us know little about: substance abuse, relationship issues, work issues; one need only to thumb through Ordinary Trauma for a glimpse of the full catalogue of its sufferings. And indeed, flashes of that younger man is still present in this collection, as in these lines from "A Solitary Theater."

> can mere thoughts
> cause your hands
> to ball into fists
> and your teeth to grind
>
> the same way
> a movie scene can
> but you're the only one
> in this theater

And again in these lines from "Making Love Easier", where the speaker is warning someone that she wouldn't like him as much as she thinks she would, were she to meet him in person:

> "My dear...
> this way's easy to take.

> Words only. Dead. You can't
> hear my tone, can't see my
> eyes dart about the room like
> vandals seeking something to smash,
> as I rave about things that can't be fixed—
> not now, not ever."

But where one reviewer commented, speaking of his earlier poems, "You have to look long and hard to find hope," you will not miss the presence of hope in this new collection. The Rihlmann of the present collection has begun to put his sufferings in perspective. For example, he begins to compare his sufferings to the sufferings of others. In "A Grumpy Guy," the speaker says,

> why couldn't I have had
> your horrors
> and your abuse?
>
> your better reasons
> for madness?
>
> I need a more valid excuse
> for those times
> when I punch holes in walls
> when I scream
> and chase people in traffic
> when I go to pieces
> over a sink full of dishes

And in a poem that might have been placed at the end of the collection, had it been ordered chronologically, called "Another Go", the speaker looks forward positively to how things may be different in his next life.

> I'd like another go at it, I think...

come back around
as less of a malcontent

    Yet even readers of Rihlmann's previous collection will not be surprised to discover he is capable of this kind of development. There, as throughout his poems here, his tone was always candid, matter-of-fact and totally free of self-pity. "The mature, well considered ponderings of a fucked-up soul wanting to salvage some good out of his life," according to one reviewer. Rihlmann's sympathy for others, trapped like himself in the mindless jobs that more and more characterize work in this country, struck a note of hope. One cannot be so lost himself who is able to feel compassion for the sufferings of others.

    Now Rihlmann proves his "mixed-up" life has yielded some growth. He is one who has come through the dark. We find him beginning to look for meaning behind the difficulties of life, as in this extraordinary poem, "Big Questions:"

In the mountains
the wind blows
on its way somewhere

a squirrel runs
across a snowfield
risking the hawk's talons

beneath the white crust
a stream trickles
toward the river

a gnarled old cedar
grows from the rocks
its roots twisted deep
beneath its branches sits a man

> scribbling big questions
> in tattered pages
>
> his black ink laid down
> like a trail of popcorn
> eaten by crows

Here like a medieval diptych past and future combine in one image: a squirrel risking its life on one panel, while on the other a saint-like figure writes his questions, questions already conditioned by "tattered pages" and the inexorable predations of nature.

This spirituality is one of Rihlmann's greatest growths to date, for like sunlight glinting through the canopy of a forest, his nascent hope opens a space in this collection for more than one poem to step out of the speaker's life, achieving a timeless and unconfined relevance. Here is "Ode to the Discarded" that shows Rihlmann to be a poet of the first order:

> While sitting on the curb,
> I see a rusty old bolt
> lying on the pavement.
>
> I pick it up,
> turn it and feel
> its heft,
> its cold edges,
> my fingers
> now stained orange.
>
> I run fingertips
> over threads
> still sharp,
> not stripped.

## NIGHT AT MY THROAT

It once held
something together,

and still could.

The title poem, "The Night at My Throat" is one of these poems. It is a poem that satisfies both emotionally and realistically, standing as it does as the hard-won culmination of the uplifting movement one has sensed in this collection all along. In this poem, the speaker faces a situation familiar to many of us, awake in the middle of the night, unable to sleep. But this moment immediately transcends our recognition as we realize the image is also of one who has awakened out of a darkness that symbolizes life. And as anyone knows who has lain awake in the dark, awareness is not always a welcome or comfortable state.

Two remedies confront us here: to turn our back on the world in a life of pure asceticism, or to allow ourselves to be called again to the neon attractions of a life of the senses. Our speaker rejects both, however—and in an act of radical self-acceptance, steps outside to look at the " few / dim / stars ", which is all that is available to him within the orbit of his life; a spiritual view no less, but conditioned by the limits of his own physical existence.

This moment is what we came here for. My summary doesn't begin to exhaust the poem's possible meanings. Each will find something within themselves to bring to it.

As the final measure of Rihlmann's achievement as a poet and a human being, I would set Rihlmann's "No Matter What you Say" from the Yellow Bird section of this book, against Yeats's "Sailing to Byzantium." Where Yeats longs to be reincarnated as a jeweled mechanical bird, as his speaker states in the last stanza of "Sailing to Byzantium," to sing to lords and ladies:

Once out of nature I shall never take
My bodily form from any natural thing,

> But such a form as Grecian goldsmiths make
> Of hammered gold and gold enamelling
> To keep a drowsy Emperor awake;
> Or set upon a golden bough to sing
> To lords and ladies of Byzantium

Rihlmann's speaker says only:

> the tiniest yellow bird
> perches in the sycamore
>
> it sings a beautiful song
> a varied and indescribable song
>
> a song I've never heard
> it sings for me
>
> it sings for me…yes—
> no matter what you say
>
> there have been mornings
> I might have yelled—
>
> what the hell have you got
> to sing about?
>
> but this is not one of them
> this is not one of them, and
>
> I think I'd like to come back
> as that—as the tiniest

# NIGHT AT MY THROAT

yellow bird, who sings
to the people going into work

who'll sing to the people
who will work in these buildings

when I'm gone
who'll sing a beautiful

and varied and indescribable song
to their frantic and worried souls

who'll sing to them...even
if they curse or throw stones

to come back and sing like that—
yes...I think I will

This is the last poem in *Night at My Throat*. This is Brian Rihlmann: Yeats a mechanical toy, Rihlmann a yellow song-bird—who sings even for those who would curse it. Let us set these two poems side by side in our minds, and let us be grateful for this book.

David Churchill
August, 2020

# DARK DREAM

## Another Go

I'd like another go at it, I think...
come back around
as less of a malcontent
someone without so much
of a bone to pick about the givens
the boundaries
the painful strings that tug
with every attempted move beyond
someone without a second mouth
to chatter and dissect
without its little piranha teeth
to gnaw every small happiness
and spit it back in their faces
like chewing gum
drained of all its flavor
someone occasionally with
and not always against
someone with faith
to leap the broad, ugly ditch
someone who lives
as though this life were a blessing
and not an inconvenience
someone less like a midwinter bear
awakened early to the icy world
from peaceful sleep, dreams
of springtime and sunshine

## Amen

I see her in the grocery store
swollen with child and glowing
just like they say, and it's true
I can't help smiling but it quickly fades
under a slow avalanche of dread
so I say this useless prayer—
may you grow straight as a green sapling
tall enough to look your peers in the eyes
may you be without a limp or stutter
or deformity to draw the pack's attention
may your soul have elephant skin
may you fight your battles against the living
and not wage futile ones against ghosts
may you live more in the tangible world
than roam monstrous dreams or nightmares
and become forever entangled there
and may you never feel the urge to write
a better life than the one you live

## A Younger Version

inside an oval frame
that hangs dustless
and polished
on the wall
of his mother's house
a smooth cheeked
younger version
bloomed with angst
amidst a thicket
of familial smiles
the eyes blazed
with dark fire
the jaw was set
against the punches
he knew were coming

## Beyond Pale Suburbia

It would've been reasonable
to go to college
and while I was there
to meet my future bride
we'd have waited to get married
until we were established in our careers
and financially secure
able to make the car payments
the mortgage

then we'd have planned
for children...two
the perfect number
a boy and a girl
if we were lucky enough

it would've been more reasonable
than to follow
such a long and tortuous path
the path of whoring
and drunkenness
and agony
that I did choose

but that dark dream
was what drew me
what whispered to me
promising life beyond pale suburbia

all through my teenage years
like a wild beast alive in the night

and so
I let that alternate version
of myself gladly suffocate
in some parallel universe
scratching at the lid
of his coffin

## Rattle

a rattle
and I turn
as a bottle
spins to a halt
mid-street
flipped like a tiddlywink
by the tire
of a passing car

I walk over
and pick it up—
vodka
the cheapest
like I used to buy
every morning
retch at the first swig
but it stopped the shaking

Its plastic body is flattened
cracked
its crushed lips
will never again
sing a hollow song

## He's Harmless

we've all seen them
those of us who live in neighborhoods
where such things are allowed
that is...

we've seen them
as they circle the block
talk to themselves
smile, laugh at nothing
occasionally yell and scream
or shadow fight with invisible demons

we say they're harmless
but we give them plenty of room
like we give those parts of ourselves
that do these things

we cross over
pass on the opposite sidewalk
don't make eye contact
he may want to talk awhile

but then they catch us unawares
after we've wandered into some blind alley
they come close, too close
stare at us with big starving eyes
like empty bowls waiting to be filled

## Surviving Home

No…you don't—you don't have
to be a loner or an outcast to write
poetry...but it helps. It certainly helps
to have been rejected enough to
take the sharp inward hairpin, and
look around at what's in here. I'd
never have done it, had I known.
Did I turn the wheel? I'm not sure.
Maybe so, but looking back it seems
like someone might've turned all the
road signs, set up some orange cones,
some neon arrows, as a sort of joke,
to lead me down a road into this
labyrinth which has become home...
a cluttered, dank, and baffling place,
though it's probably where I'm supposed
to be, if I'm supposed to be anywhere,
that is. Maybe I can show others how to
survive this kind of home, if not to thrive
here. That remains to be seen.

# THE ONE LESS SOUL

## Memories

they say the body remembers...
remembers trauma, for example
and it's interesting
that for me, anxiety lodges itself
like a big empty balloon
pressing against my upper abdomen
the solar plexus
just below the heart—
the exact spot
a bully might take his shot
to knock the wind out of you
leave you gasping on the floor
while all his disciples laugh
maybe it's a little lower, now
maybe it's sagged a bit
over the years

## Calling The Wolves

her name was Emma
she called me "the little fella"
wore a patch
over one side of her glasses
to cover the droopy eye
didn't talk much

but I liked her old house
on Arch Street in Butler
built on stilts into a hillside
my matchbox cars
rolled on their own
across the faded green linoleum

the place she lived later—
I hated that place
the Lysol smell
mixed with diapers
piss and shit

the woman down the hall
who bleated inconsolably
as a lost and wounded sheep
wandering in darkness

did she not realize her cries
would bring the wolves?

maybe she was calling them
to take her away

maybe all the others
were ready to go too

maybe that's why nobody
ever shut her up

## A Long Life

Dad walked up to me
in the backyard looking sad
put a hand on my shoulder
and told me she'd died
and I said "oh"
not knowing what else to say

I felt nothing, particularly
just an odd solemn silence
I remember how everyone
talked more quietly
moved more slowly
I guessed that was the thing to do
I tried to follow their steps
to play along

at the funeral mom and I approached
her casket and stood there, looking in
she appeared clownish, unnatural
her thin hair fluffed
her cheeks too red
but beneath, she was gray

Mom looked tired as she
stared at her own grandmother
sighed, and said,
"Well....she lived a long life"
and even then, I remember thinking
"But not a very happy one"

## Contrast

the day of the night you
died, we were there—
three of us were there,
others weren't...
too busy for the tedium of dying,
I guess

my uncle stared
from across the room
but came no closer
he left after a few minutes
while Mom and I stayed,
whispered things, memories

you peered at us through the slit
of your good eye,
on the non-stroke side,
drew letters in the air
with your good hand
C-O-L-D
cold...I finally understood,
added another blanket

I stayed longer
than Mom, that day...
I think I knew

I sat with you,
listened to you breathe,

held mine
when a pause came

I wondered if you knew
what was happening,
if you were scared

I wished it quickly for you
and also not at all

while you slept again, I
sat in the outside garden,
wandered the halls alone

in a waiting area
sat a large family—
15-20 people...
adults, teenagers, children...
discussing who would stay
that evening
and later that night,
making plans,
taking shifts

I eavesdropped
just enough,
then swallowed
the rough edges
of the contrast,

# NIGHT AT MY THROAT

and walked back
to your room

## "Here Comes The Airplane!"

there's a problem
with being the one
who always smells it
with being the one
who always turns up your nose
and clamps your lips tight
as life's mouth
hums airplane noises
and its hand
orbits your head
with a spoonful of bullshit
like Mom did
with the bland
unflavored oatmeal
enticing you
to open wide
and take a bite...
because sometimes bullshit
is all there is
and it's either that
or starve

## How Do You Want Your Eggs?

last night as my marble eyes
rolled and twitched in their sockets
you appeared to me, withered
in your hospital bed

I gathered your bones in my arms
I embraced you like I hadn't,
that day, when I thought
there'd be another time

I held you and whispered
how I'd quit drinking, finally,
like you always pestered me

you half smiled
with the good side of your mouth
breathed a last breath and vanished

I held the empty bedsheets, confused
as the scene became your kitchen
where a restored you stood at the stove

your hair was dark and thick
your face the same age
as when I first met you
and grabbed your finger with my tiny hand

you turned to me
at the kitchen table
smiled, and asked—
"How do you want your eggs?"

## Like It Was

I haven't seen or talked to you
in five years
but last night in a dream
you stood before me
chubby and pale
awkward and pimply
like back in high school
not steroid pumped
tattooed and tanned like now
and you cry
because she's gone
and I put my arm around you
like a friend
like a brother
like it was
before social media
before we were so "connected"
before we knew anything
about right/left politics
and the world
and how messed up
things can get
back when we knew everything
or at least something more
than we do now

## One Less Soul

Nan always worried
about me being alone—
when she still lived in Florida
she tried fixing me up
with a young nurse
at her doctor's office
showed her my picture
gave her my email address

(never mind the couple thousand miles
between us...)

poor old woman—
she actually thought
I'd be a great catch
for some pretty young thing

she died believing that

now I see
what a shame it is
to not have her around
to believe such a thing

to have one less soul
out in the world
so deluded about me

## Riding The Ride

down on the Jersey shore
one summer
(I was maybe five)
I begged her
to let me ride the ride

it resembled
a miniature roller coaster
with shiny red cars

the people climbed off
looking breathless and happy

she finally said ok
we climbed into the little two seater
and buckled up
the man hit the lever
I smiled

before long I was screaming
and wailing
to let me off this thing
but all she could do
was wrap her arm
tighter around me
as we careened over hills
and around corners faster
faster than I'd ever imagined possible

time dilated like terrified eyes
but eventually we slowed
and came to rest

until the man pushed another lever
and we began to roll again
backwards this time

through the whole ordeal

I had no understanding
of metaphor
yet

## The First Noble Truth Of Wobbly

dukkha is the word
translated as suffering
but they say the original meaning
referred to the empty axle hole
of a wheel—a bad fit
makes for a bumpy ride

I think of hard landings
from bicycle jumps
and riding around on bent rims

I'd try to tighten the spokes myself
but I never got it right
and just made it more wobbly
dad would sigh, growl...
and drive me to the bike shop

and now...
after 125 thousand miles
I think a bearing is starting to go
on my old Chevy—
the center not holding
and all that jazz

I've been driving it for weeks
while keeping an ear
on the grumbling sound
emitting from the front wheel
like a voice of protest

guess I'll have to
take it in soon
take it to someone
with the right tools

It was my grandma's car
I bought it from her back in 2010
when macular degeneration
darkened the center of her vision

and then four years ago
a stroke and pneumonia
took her away

no one had the tools
to fix that
though they wanted to try...
plug her full of tubes
she shook her head, "No"

the earth wobbles
on its axis, too
you know

## The Whole Point Of The Game

the headline of the article
said something about
dodgeball being dehumanizing
he ridiculed it, of course
this "friend" of mine
said we're turning
our kids into a bunch of pussies
blah, blah, blah
and though I didn't read it
it brought back memories
of those rainy days
in Junior High
when I last played the game...

how some poor kid
smaller or weaker
or fatter or bookish
was always singled out
while we—
like little savages out of Golding—
all pegged him at once
usually aiming for the face
a bloody nose
or broken glasses
was glorious
and celebrated with
high fives and riotous laughter

I'm sure
for the rest of the day
those kids sat in class
with swollen, bee-stung faces
and pondered the sin
of being smaller
or weaker
or fatter
or bookish

and did this toughen them up
and help them become
happy and well-adjusted adults?

I could ask
but it's the damnedest thing...
we haven't kept in touch

## Vertigo

a father
spins his little girl
on a merry go round
at the park
as she squeals
and yells "faster"
and finally disembarks
dizzy and falling down
but laughing
and I remember
doing the same
as a boy
on a backyard tire swing
and how I loved
the vertigo
the drunken feel
of the world
turned upside down
now I feel like that
most of the time
but I don't laugh at it
anymore

## Michelle

you went with the blonde haired boy
with the beautiful blue glass eye
and the fair skin
although I smiled at you in class
called you on the phone
and rode my bike past your house
a hundred
a thousand times
dripping with sweat
in the buzzing locust summer
and didn't you know I was there?
you must have known...
how could you not hear
my pulse racing
every time it passed outside
your shuttered window?
how could my teenage desires
not rule over everything
there ever was
or would be?
but your window remained closed
as I finally circled around
mid-street
stared one last time
and pedaled home
through the tall twilight shadows
of sagging suburban trees

## Pusillanimous

there are times
yes, oftentimes...
when the soul is small—
tiny as the boy
kicked down the stairs
for the sin of being literally less
in this material world

ask the squirrel
and the sparrow
about their darting eyes
and their secretive ways

ask the boy
why he loves
those silly ninja movies
so much

why he dreams
of those graceful assassins
moving invisibly, noiselessly
through the night

cloaked in black
deadly swords gleaming
in dark scabbards

how they vanish
before their enemies

in a haze of smoke
in hallways...locker rooms...
wherever

he'd love to be able
to do that

## Survivor

on a chilly October evening
a lone dandelion
gone to seed
stands in the midst
of a green field

its puffy head
having somehow
survived the whirling blades
of a recent mowing

it stands stiffly tall
a white haired old man
awaiting immortality
in a gust of wind
or a child's wish

# DANCE OF TOUCH

## A Box Of Scraps

I look at this box
full of yellow sticky notes
and scraps of paper

not to mention
all the notebooks and digital files
crammed with forgotten poems

thousands of words
that'll probably die with me
and maybe they should

I'll never finish all this
and that makes me
sink just a little

until I consider
all the times
I've strummed my guitar

for no one's ears
but mine, and then—
I float back to the surface

## Big Questions

In the mountains
the wind blows
on its way somewhere

a squirrel runs
across a snowfield
risking the hawk's talons

beneath the white crust
a stream trickles
toward the river

a gnarled old cedar
grows from the rocks
its roots twisted deep

beneath its branches sits a man
scribbling big questions
in tattered pages

his black ink laid down
like a trail of popcorn
eaten by crows

## Heart

I thought I'd write my
heart out, you know?
Empty it, pour it down the
drain like spoiled milk.
But heart's not in us...we're in IT.
And there's no outside,
and no other side.
It's all a giant, pulsing heart.
You don't empty that.
And you never know it—
how fish don't know the ocean.
They only swim in it.
Through it.
Are filled with it.
They only see light and shadow,
only feel warmth and cold,
the tug of currents,
the pull of the moon
and its tides.

## Dream Of A Love

I'd never have gotten along
in a purely oral culture,
one without a written language.
Talking's too messy, ugly.
We stutter and stumble.
We overlap, argue, begin to shout...
shower each other with spittle.
Blink away the words
and the wounds beneath.
No...
I dream of a love
where we seldom converse,
but instead communicate
through a dance of touch,
body language
and semaphore gazes.
We'd write little poems
on post it notes.
Leave them around the house.
On the bathroom mirror.
In the cupboard.
Hide them like Easter eggs.
We'd wear colors to indicate mood,
sleep in separate bedrooms sometimes,
if we clashed too much,
but with understanding,
and without grudge.
The night's silence a blessing,
not a bludgeon.

## Acceptance

I wrote it without a problem.
But now as I sit alone in my room,
as the dim sunrise creeps in...
as I read it aloud,
and breathe life into its body, I shiver.
My voice cracks.
I stop reading as a tear flows,
and as I wipe it away I think, yes....
yes, this one will be taken.
These strangers will have me.
Onscreen, on the page...
they will take every bit
of two-dimensional me.

# THE CLEAR BLUE
# THAT'S ALWAYS THERE

## Making Love Easier

An online friend, a younger woman
with a closet full of black says
she loves my brutal honesty...
even my grouchiness
and my irascibility.
I want to tell her the truth, to say—

"My dear...
what you love in the abstract
you would despise in its embodiment."

"My dear...
this way's easy to take.
Words only.  Dead. You can't
hear my tone, can't see my
eyes dart about the room like
vandals seeking something to smash,
as I rave about things that can't be fixed—
not now, not ever."

"My dear...
though you believe
you could love me
and live with this at close range,
I assure you—
you could not.
Not even I can...
though I do."

I'd tell her this
but she wouldn't believe it,
and right now...
a love distant and dark,
a love that dances at light speed,
a love that teases through
cables and screens,
the shimmering appearance
and possibility of love
that winks at me like a
faraway and perhaps dead star
is better than nothing—
and much better than a flame
of female hatred, here
in my matchstick house.

## A Dumb Question

we meet for coffee
once a month
lately she's fixated
on the meaning of it all
the big stuff
you know?

when she asks "Why?"
I say "that's a dumb question!"
we're old friends
so she laughs

then I throw
a little Alan Watts her way
"the meaning of life
is simply to be alive"

she nods, ponders that

I am a Zen master, a guru
I am enlightened
I have the answers
or better yet—
I am beyond the questions

we drink our coffee
talk for an hour
until I've got to leave for work

we hug, say goodbye
"next month?"
"you bet!"

invariably
in a week or two
or later that same evening
I'll find myself
either pounding the earth
and shouting
or huddled in a corner
and whispering
that same dumb question

## A Grumpy Guy

i sat at my work desk today
headphones in
listening to your story

and several times
had to quit typing
to wipe my eyes
and shiver

later
as i thought about it
you grew larger
while i shrank

why couldn't i have had
your horrors
and your abuse?

your better reasons
for madness?

i need a more valid excuse
for those times
when i punch holes in walls
when i scream
and chase people in traffic
when i go to pieces
over a sink full of dishes

more than a diagnosis
most perceive
as simple weakness
an "attitude problem"
a farce
or dramatic streak

("his parents should have
beaten him more")

to the world
that sees the surface
i'm just an asshole
or a grumpy guy

that ties me up
in a neat bow
and they go on
with their lives

while i wriggle
against the straitjacket
of their strutting certainty

## A Solitary Theater

how can mere thoughts
cause your hands
to ball into fists
and your teeth to grind

the same way
a movie scene can
but you're the only one
in this theater

you look for the door
there isn't one

you snip the film
it sews itself together

you hack the projector cable
it grows back
like a lizard's tail

you describe the horror
of the scene for the others

they squint
yawn
or laugh

## Anything But This

I'd rather be anything
but this oak tree—
a gnarled old thing, half-rotted
nothing but layers of secrets
wrapped in secrets
awaiting the blade
and revelation

years of sickness
years of drought or infestation
carved initials inside hearts
now returned to the soil
barbed wire absorbed
rusty nails embedded in its flesh

deep—a black layer
fire scars concealed yet remembered
and above, last year's withered leaves
still cling to the branches
and hiss when the wind blows
the dead, once more
speak louder than the living

## Around The Corner

around the corner
from the office
grows a blackberry
and a rose bush
both covered with thorns
buds in various stages—
tight green, just unfolding
or bursting wide

soon the people will arrive
sit in their cars
gather at the door
or pace the parking lot

they'll crack jokes
bitch about the weather
or stand silently and wait
for the boss to unlock the door
eyes shut
headphones in

from my curbside seat
around the corner
next to the blackberry
and the rose bush
I hear their voices fade
as they go inside
I wait a moment
then follow

## Be Still, Now

why, this baffling heaviness?
when you expected buoyancy, or flight?
because—
it's a loss, man...a loss
another thing gone
and no matter what you say
or what THEY say
no matter what you think you've learned
or how hard you imagine you've become
it'll never NOT bother you
how these things go
how they always turn out

remember how you freaked out
when you dropped your keys in the river?
remember the rush, the relief,
when you found them again?

well....this is bigger

so let it bother you awhile, then
let it sit heavy on your chest like a vulture
let it do its thing to your heart
and let it go when it's ready

quit flailing your arms
and scaring it off

# NIGHT AT MY THROAT

you'll tire, eventually
and it'll be back

see it circling?

## Bear Trap

he had two Master's degrees
and I had nothing
but a couple of classes
and a head full of books

as we drank whiskey
and talked one day
in his flophouse room
about history and philosophy
he stopped, looked at me
and growled, in his way:
"You got a mind
like a fuckin' bear trap, kid!"

he had no idea
how right he was
because in the years since
these jaws have grabbed
many things
more dangerous
than an ursine beast

things that have done
more damage
than mere teeth
and claws
ever could

and still
they hold on

## Between Man And Beast

my earplugs are in
so I don't hear him
don't notice as he
sits at the other end
of the long table

until I feel the vibrations
across 8 feet of hardwood—
the pounding of his middle fingers
on the keys
like angry little fists

I stare until he
looks up, then away
continues to pound

he either does
or doesn't understand
what the look is about

I clench my jaw
against the words
kicking the backs
of my teeth
and try to work
try to finish the poem
I'm writing

a hundred times a day
I'm called to reconcile
what I'd like to do
with what's socially acceptable
but there's no reconciling them—

I can only squirm
in this wretched gap
where I live

## Break

some days you go
into the employee bathroom
lock the door
and wrap your arms
around yourself
for awhile

it feels pretty good—
warm
you could stay here
like this…

sometimes you stay
for longer
than you should

and no one yells
or pounds the door
but then something
kicks you into motion
like an automaton

you break yourself
from yourself
from your own arms
like a lover
who's having second thoughts

you walk to the sink
hands on the cold porcelain
you lean in
look your mirror self
almost
in the eye

then turn away
and go back out
into the real world
the gray world
the tick-tock
timeclock
world

## Caught In The Groove

A bright summer's day
trapped outside my window.
I peer from under blankets,
as a love song echoes
in my mind.

Notes drift through
shadows shifting
on the walls,
a sad melody,
the needle caught
in the groove.

I roll in twisted sheets
stare at the ceiling
then shut my eyes,
sleep off the day's music
like a hangover.

But each time I wake,
notes wash over me,
again,
like your ghost.

You're not dead,
but lost
in a time I cannot grasp,
or understand,
a time I was loved.

## Cobwebs

there are cobwebs
in the hallway now
others tell me
I am the spider—
they insist on it
though I barely remember
spinning them

there must have been
a good reason
these traps must have
kept me safe, once
when I huddled
at the dead end
my back to the wall
listening for who
or what
was surely coming

now they rustle
with dead leaves
they disturb my sleep
and invade my dreams
they catch nothing
but orphaned seeds
and the occasional fly
whose frantic, angry buzz
sounds more and more
like my own voice
the longer I listen

## Codependency In The Social Media Age

it burrows persistently
this worm of what I owe
to those I know
only by words
avatars
photos

have I returned
enough kindness?
have I sent
enough smiles?

how many more hearts
do I have in my pocket
buried under lint
and old pennies?

it chews and chews
until my soul
is a honeycomb
paper thin cells
collapsing

I wonder if
Salinger's old house
is for sale
in the deep north woods

I'll shut myself up there
or someplace like it
until winter
until there's no escape
on the snowbound roads

I'll break myself
of this habit
this junkie obsession

but then
I'll just wind up
conjuring gods
or demons to appease

and I do that anyway

## Coffee Mug

it's seven years old, now
and we've been history for six
but I still drink from it, daily
it's the one thing I still have
that you bought for me

the lid still seals
and keeps my coffee warm—
for awhile

but no lid
keeps things warm forever

it's not so pretty anymore—
it's dented on the bottom
it wobbles

about a quarter
of the red coating
has chipped away
exposing the stainless steel beneath

it shines naked
in the coffeehouse lights
as I tap these words

maybe....
maybe once all that red is gone

flaked away like ashes
I'll get rid of it

maybe once it's all worn off
then...
you'll be gone too

## Conman

12 hours in bed
asleep or partially so
and still a second gravity
tugs at my orbit
as I make coffee
contemplating the normal
futile routine

the flame is dim
the words are stupid
to be recognized
for piling them up
is obscene

I'm a clown
a conman
a televangelist
without scruples
who knows
that the god he peddles
is a fraud

I carry these blank tablets
down from the mountain
and pretend to read them—

a message of bewilderment
and discontent
as though THAT

BRIAN RIHLMANN

was something unique
something profound
or salvific

## Control Freak

sometimes
after a few restless nights
I get a real good sleep
8-9 hours
like death and rebirth
and I awaken refreshed
but so is he—
the nemesis
he comes out swinging
an ultimate fighter on speed

after he pummels me awhile
with the bony knuckles
of the past
he's eager to talk
about all he's seen
about every disaster
that awaits me
in the near
or distant future

he's a time traveler
and clairvoyant too
he's read the minds
of all my friends, coworkers
and even strangers—
"you won't BELIEVE
what that guy just said
about you!"

yep
he knows it all
just ask him
he'll tell ya!
there's no room
in his world
for "wait and see"
he's got the bridge
the wheel
the puppet strings

the whole goddamn
chess board
and all the pieces...
it's all his!

## Conversations

You can tell yourself
that all this head trouble
is just clouds obscuring the sky;
the clear blue that's always there
beyond the swirl,

just like you told yourself
that she still loved you,
despite the late nights,
and those strange looks
you'd never seen before,

or that you still loved her
as you sat on the couch
after midnight,
having a third cocktail,
plotting your escape.

## Deadly

many people are offended
by the smell of cigarette smoke
but it doesn't bother me
as I sit here
outside the coffeehouse
on a windless morning
three tables down
watching her
the way she holds her cigarette
in the same hand
she taps at her phone with
and how the blue-gray fingers of smoke
caress her face
before drifting into
the brilliant sunlight
and vanishing
and I can't help
but admire its beauty
like the beauty
of cobras, tigers
and all dangerous
and deadly things
and all things are
finally
deadly

## Drained

I have a thing about that, too—
people seeing the title
of the book I'm reading

it's too much of a window
without a shade
might invite conversation from strangers—
the horror

but she sits with it on display
as though she wants us to see—
"The Subtle Art Of Not Giving A Fuck!"

I know the book
I've read excerpts
I get the point

I too, give many fucks
where fucks should not
be given

leaving me drained
for the important things
like—

like I don't know what

like actual fucking maybe?

I'd say love
but I've been drained of that
for years

a series of vampires
lovely...dark...
deadly as nightshade

## Embarrassment

when I am praised
and the praise is genuine
my mind goes blank
as though a great teacher
had just presented
an impenetrable riddle

I look away
toward the floor
or the sky
as I sweep a spotlight
across my inner emptiness
seeking a way out—
a rebuttal
a joke
or some other way
to disappear

I squirm and stutter
and pollute the air
with the sound of my voice
when I should merely bow
shake his hand
and leave the room
without a word

## Eviction

You've been a squatter
for far too long here,
my dear.

Just look at this place!
You've really made
a mess of it.

I clear out your bedding,
sweep the ashes
of your fires away,
and padlock the door, again.

I hid the key
under the mat.

## Except

she said she loved my nihilism
the way my poems
seemed to do to love
what a boot does
to the pinched off
glowing end of a cigarette

and I said—
I'm not a nihilist
no one really is
I wish I were
I wish love WAS a useless
and meaningless thing—
a dead stalk of a winter weed
that could be hacked away
and forgotten

I've tried—
I told her
but another springtime always comes
with its tilt toward the sun
its damned warmth and rain

those thirsty roots
drink it down, and again
that deadly flower rears like a lion's head
from the frozen ground
it shows its teeth

it roars
it terrifies

it rends to ribbons the tinfoil armor
with which we've shrouded our wary hearts
it returns to do this
as surely as death
it comes despite our lack of faith
our skepticism
about any reality lurking
beneath the mask
of that cursed four letter word

I said too much
and that was the end
she remains silent
she might have loved me…
except.

## Flypaper

when you're kinda sticky
no matter how you scrub
no matter how you coat
or oil yourself

when a minor upset
can buzz around for days
and a major one
for years
for a lifetime....
(lifetimes?)

you tend to avoid the potential
the places where flies gather
warm bodies

you cultivate
the mean mug
and the dagger stare
practice in your mirror
Travis Bickle style

not out of malice
but to keep the cushion
of no man's land
you need to survive

later you learn to avoid
phone calls, emails,

social media
before bed

an angry message
from a jilted follower
blocked on the grounds
of being an insane
and racist asshole

you hole up
in various caves and closets
in cocoons spun
by a fevered imagination

## Frozen

you may get
more than one shot
at a lot of things—
at jobs, success,
love or money

another chance to stand up
and climb whatever hill
you've tumbled down

but it can only happen once
that you go online
and stumble upon photos
of a crush from 20 years ago
and see how
rough country life
has etched her

and scroll
to find her daughter
grown now
with three kids of her own

the face of her mother
at twenty-two
smiles
and you are frozen
chills and all

## Getting Over, Getting Under

Her breasts swayed inside
her blouse as she moved around
behind the bar, wiping things
with a dirty rag and telling me
"You know...they say the best
way to get over a man is
to get under another one."

We laughed at that, and before I
could say, "you know...." (wink, wink)
"I could help you out there..."
I said instead, "Isn't that like
drinking to cure a hangover?"

And she laughed, said "Maybe so.
It works, though, right?" I
smiled, nodded, and slid my
empty glass across the bar.
She took it, with a flourish
and a twirl, broke out the vodka,
the tomato juice, the Worcestershire...

She mixed us two spicy, bloody ones,
and our eyes met as we
clinked glasses in a
silent toast to getting over,
or under. That was all that
ever happened, but how beautifully

## NIGHT AT MY THROAT

the smoke from our cigarettes
rose and intertwined in
the too-bright flood of morning sun
pouring in through the window.

## Heaviness

Saturday. I awaken again to the
familiar inertia.  Even my fingertips
are leaden, as I tap these words.
A trip to the coffee shop seems like
crossing the Khyber.  Faces, mouths,
smiles.  The awful, contrasting joy.
All their laughter directed at the
punch line my life has become.

I should snap out of it. Slap myself
in the face two, three times—hard!
I should shave.  Go for a walk.  Get out
among the people of the world.  Make
some contribution, instead of just lying
here, rotting.  A vegetable, not a man.

An hour passes. Maybe I should see a
doctor.  Maybe there's a benign tumor,
that's making the air seem so heavy,
and "we don't even need to saw
your skull open....there's a drug that
dissolves it, you'll be good as new!"

I'll pop back open.  I'll even feel like
loving again.  I'll sign up on that dating
site and not cringe at every stupid question.
I'll write a glowing review of myself and
all my positive qualities.  None of it falsified.

I'll smile for the camera, and it'll be
a genuine smile…just you wait!

I go back to sleep. Out of reach
of dreams and recriminations. I awaken
at noon and shuffle to the fridge.
Nothing. I'll have to leave the house.

## Hoarder

I used to watch shows
about hoarders
and think my god....
how can you live
like that?
in houses filled
with rats or cats
in houses packed
with the accumulated junk
of a lifetime
in houses with plumbing
that doesn't work anymore
so you shit in plastic bags
and throw them in the basement

I mean
what the fuck
is wrong
with you people?

but now
two plus years sober
as I daily navigate
the junkyard and sewer
of my own mind
scraping congealed puddles
of who knows what
off the floor

## NIGHT AT MY THROAT

under white hot spotlights
of teetotaler awareness...

I don't wonder
about that anymore

## I Die Anyway

appalled
by the terms
of the contract
I snatch it
from your desk
and strike a match

and I laugh
as it burns
until I see
the teardrop
on your cheek
the dulled shine
of your sad dog eyes

the flame rages
sucks the oxygen
from the room
and I die anyway
despite my refusal to sign

I die anyway
choking on the ashes
bitter and gray
as you sigh
and finally turn away

## I Smile

soon I'll hear
the last cricket
of summer
sing his song
to the chilly night

and I'll think
of the last man
or the last woman

there will be one
someday
you know

I imagine myself
in their place

and wonder
what my song
would sound like
or if I'd sing at all

tonight I sit in my room
alone and listen
through the open window

fewer but still several
fiddling in the dark

for now
I smile

## Karma Machines

as we squeeze the wild things
into smaller spaces
and find bears roaming our streets

so we must find a place
amid the growing shadows
of our adolescent creation

we bow to its demands
scramble to match its stride
vanish in pixelated seas

our faces become clocks
our souls the spinning hands
our eyes reflect the screen's glare

we are moons to its sun
satellites locked in orbit
around an ever increasing mass

there's no room
for wobbles of spontaneity
this is our chosen path

we march toward destiny
our footsteps measured
as the movement of pistons

inspired by these role models
we relish a more efficient humanity
our eyes adore the new pantheon

## Living With This And That

what can we say, really?
I am this way
and you are that way...

your that sends my this
scurrying up the wall
into some dark corner
while my this
twists your face
into a mask
of bewildered devastation

my this sulks and skulks
in its hiding spot
it peers out
it sees the damage
but can do nothing, nothing....

all the words it could speak
are utterly useless...
as useless
as these

## Loose Ends

It's Saturday afternoon
and you have
done the shopping
washed the car
and mowed the lawn

the grass stands in neat rows
square at the edges
indicating to passers by
that you've really
got your act together

but inside
you sit crying
on the sofa
and pour yourself
another round

as on screen lovers reunite
and tie up that bow—
those loose ends
you cannot find anywhere

## More Than

there is no now
or there is only now
as I pace circles
at the bottom
of this silo

as I touch its walls
and pack the earth
hard as a tombstone
beneath my soles

nothing to do
nowhere to go
there was a ladder once
and a door
but they're gone now
I don't know where

I just pace
and chew my nails
mumble meaningless words
to the uncomprehending darkness

I know
outside these walls
there's a truck backing up
a behemoth with a bellyful
ready to rain
a mountain on me

and maybe
it already has
maybe I was asleep
and dreaming
when it happened

because there's more
than just air in here
a whole heavy world
of "more than"
in here

## My Accomplice

just before I turn off the light
I see a spider crawling
along the molding

I envision him biting me
or crawling in my mouth
as I sleep

I move to squash him
but then I stop
and instead imagine
that he might sneak in through my ear
undetected
and spin a web in my brain

he'll clear out the tangles
and create something symmetrical
something orderly
from the chaos
an honest to god dreamcatcher
the real thing
not like this useless talisman
that dangles above me
empty

you'll fly straight into it
and get caught

he'll wrap you up
in a little cocoon
and bring you to me

don't squirm, my love...
I won't hurt you
this time

## My Greatest Talent

long before
these purgatory days
I've kept my distance...

I've kept it in sandboxes
on the playground
in crowded hallways
and classrooms

I've kept it at bars
at parties
at concerts
and in mosh pits

I've kept it during family reunions
during therapy sessions
during group photos, group hugs
or cheek to cheek selfies

I've kept it in shared spaces
in motel rooms, apartments
in beds strange or familiar

I've kept it holding hands
and hearts
and while I was
deep inside you...
and I think you could tell—

you're gone
and far away

you learned it
from me

## My Segment

it's the feeling of
passing a semi on the
inside of a narrow curve as he
drifts toward the center and
you inch toward the guardrail and
hit the gas

endure whole days
of squeezing through like this
then ask about the indentations
my hands leave on the
steering wheel...ask
about my furrowed brow
my jumpy stare

I so want your straightaway
your 4 a.m. Sacramento freeway
five lanes...light traffic...
the smooth valley floor

but I've got this narrow stretch
through the canyon
the tightening curves
the uneven pavement
the deep snowplow scars

it's my segment of the race—

a concrete divider on one side
big wheels on the other
another set in front
spitting pebbles at my windshield
as I flinch and wait
for the gap

## My Self

I can have my self
all straightened out

all the creases ironed flat
like a pair of slacks

meticulously prepared
for an occasion

but if you ask about it
I stutter and I blush

I sweat as I plumb the pockets
under your spotlight

seeking answers like tarnished coins
buried deep in folds

as I struggle, you giggle
and resentment sprouts

like a dandelion seed
in the darkest soil

and I must withdraw
to tend my private garden

and become whole
once more

## No One Can

he comes in
ten minutes late
sits at the desk
beside mine
sighs, and says
"man....I wish it was 4 already"

I chuckle and nod
then buckle in for the ride
I tap away
break for lunch at noon
breathe a thousand breaths
think a million thoughts

about 3:30 we look at each other
he says "almost over"
I lean back in my chair, "yep"

"almost over"
is supposed to be
a good thing
in this context

yet the lives
are the days
and the hours
and the minutes

## NIGHT AT MY THROAT

I almost ask him
the obvious question
the "where does it go?" thing

but he won't be able
to answer that
no one can

it's 4...quittin' time
I punch the clock
trot out to my car
gotta get ahead
of the pack

## Ode To The Discarded

While sitting on the curb,
I see a rusty old bolt
lying on the pavement.

I pick it up,
turn it and feel
its heft,
its cold edges,
my fingers
now stained orange.

I run fingertips
over threads
still sharp,
not stripped.

It once held
something together,

and still could.

## On Reductionism

I suppose
every thought
every emotion
could be reduced
to a random discharge
nothing but electricity
bouncing around
inside our brains

same with lightning too—
just a build up
and a release
a flash
that lights the night
a sound
that splits the silence

tell this
to the blackened tree
and the burning forest

tell it to the wide eyes
fleeing the blaze
in terror

## Over Like A Song

either I wasn't quite the bastard I remember
or I have loved exceedingly forgiving women
because there's still a few exes around
who like my company

It's always the same
before I leave—
a shower first
and should I shave?
(backhanding stubble)

then on to the closet
which t-shirt?

and always, ALWAYS
I pick a tight-fitting one

I slip it on
flex in the mirror

then strip it off
and slip it back on the hanger

signals, dude…signals
it's not a date

you're not going over there
to seduce her, right?
It's over, right?

## NIGHT AT MY THROAT

It's over, yeah
over like a song's over

the last one you heard in your car
before work

the one whose melody
now echoes through your hollows
while you do your stupid job

the one that returns
later that night
after the TV's off
to fill the silent vacuum
before sleep
and dreams

## Peripheral

the hour old sun is a smear of light
across the ripples of the lake
a comet with a tail of winking fireflies
tiny sparks that flash brief and brilliant
as a murderer's knife
as newborn love, youth,
or a thousand should have beens

I stand alone on the dock...transfixed
for a moment I imagine
your hand in mine

though this is a mere reflection
like any bright light
or hideous truth
I cannot stare at it for too long
but must glance quickly
then away again

from the corner of my eye
I can look
a little bit longer

## Prosthetics

I round the aisle and nearly
bump her with my cart.  She
smiles and I smile and we both
walk on.  I turn and look—
a perfect bubble ass beneath
a short pink skirt. A smooth
leg, ivory skin.  The other's black...
plastic and shiny, tapering
into a titanium calf.

I love her...how she owns the lack.
I want to follow.  Ask if she'll
be my guru, but no—
if mine was visible, maybe.
A stump, or even a scar.  A limp.
A crutch or a cane.  Something.
All I've got is this.  Nobody can
see it, and there's no prosthetic.
No way to strut.

Though I do scribble a lot.
I've got hundreds of pages of lack—
stacks of it, propping me up.
I guess I could bring her home.
Show her that.  Watch as
realization creeps in, and her
eyes search for an exit.

## Rorschach Test

when I gaze
over the ocean
as I watch the waves
crash against the rocks
and each other
as they advance
and retreat

I see war
I see chaos and conflict
a blue beast that wrestles with itself
and neither wins nor loses
but merely struggles

beyond this myopic mirror view
is the awareness—
it's just a lot of water
sloshing around

but today my nose
is pressed against the glass
by an indomitable hand
on the back of my head

## Scream

some mornings
you awaken in a
good enough mood
to return the corporately required
"Good morning!"
of the squeaky-voiced barista
at the coffee shop

but your voice is hoarse
you croak like an old bullfrog
and don't know why

you feel your throat
palpate glands, thinking—
maybe I'm coming down with something

then you remember—
for it was less than 24 hours ago
as the vultures feasted
and their screeching reached a crescendo
how you took that unscheduled break
left the office, walked to your car
got in, shut the door
and screamed at everyone
and no one

how it was either that
or something much
much worse

## Slowly

it was after the trip East
a couple of blowups on the road
and then the chill back home
despite the muggy summer coming on

we'd gone bad
however it happens
but we would try again, soon
there was enough left
to cling to—
more than enough

I took a studio apartment
not too far away
a place to get my head right
maybe cut back on the drinking

I'd left a few odds and ends at our place
excuses I suppose

still had my key but
on the phone one day
a couple weeks after the move
you asked that I not stop by
unless you were there

It's just weird, now
you said
and I said all right

## NIGHT AT MY THROAT

I knew, then...
but I wanted more
and I got it all
when I unlocked the door

a guitar...not mine
a man's shirt, a pair of jeans
in our bedroom closet

the room became dark
and I grew dizzy
like a man who'd suddenly lost
a quart of blood

I sat on our bed
and steadied myself
as it rushed back in and filled me
and kept on coming

until I burst slowly
over the next few years

## Sobering Up

takes longer than
a day or two...

or a year

because it's not the booze
you're sobering up from

it's the infinite radius
of yourself
now collapsed
to a dot

a sharpened pencil point
wandering a vast blank page
without edges

the years of fantasies
about "who you are"
punctured and hissing
in your face

as again and again
we are dissected
by the now unblunted edge
of life's blade
that slices us open
laying bare

## NIGHT AT MY THROAT

pools of darkness
and pockets of light

the latter
often more difficult to accept
for dilated eyes
used to straining
through worlds darker
than brown glass reflections
or blackouts

## So They Say

the mind is already polished
so they say...
like a bright mirror
it has no claws
to snatch doves
or crows from the sky
no teeth
to snap their necks
yet I am filled with
their bones
I choke on their feathers
like a stray cat
a lost and homeless creature
wandering
through dark alleys
of terror

## Solstice

you read the news and ask why
I ask why not?
why not a bigger outbreak
of so-called insanity?
the sun barely above the horizon
the holiday stranglehold
the long hours on the job
sitting in traffic, again
fucked out of our bonuses, again
just generally fucked—
by bosses and landlords
by Wall Street
by politicians who know
that less is always more
where we're concerned
"You gotta want it bad!"
as we endure day after day
of one hated task after another
of slaving for evaporated dreams
of way too much yet not enough—
like how we're too fat
yet thin as an expanding balloon
of pink bubble gum
between the lips of a sullen teenager
walking on a gray morning
towards a fenced-in compound
that looks more like a prison
than a high school
it's good practice, I suppose

## Tactics

the last couple of years
I started to see gang tags
in my neighborhood too
and the guy two floors down
was slinging dope—
cars came and went
like a drive up window

then one morning I came downstairs
and my neighbor
was sweeping glass
off his front seat
with a work-gloved hand
muttering "goddamn motherfuckers"

I cleared everything out of my car
spare change, toolbox…everything
and left it unlocked
from then on

one day, soon after
I found my trunk popped
the glovebox open
owner's manual
on the front seat

I opened the door
and looked around, sniffed—
they hadn't pissed in there

## NIGHT AT MY THROAT

or carved up the interior
with a switchblade
out of frustration

and I smiled, thinking—
it's gonna be a good day

## Talk About A Mess!

I've often despised the chaos here—
how she can destroy a pristine house
and undo hours of organizing
in minutes

yet my reluctance to leave
should be no surprise—

the trail of wreckage
is something to wag my finger at
especially on ugly mornings
when my razor soul
sees the blank slate
of a bright new day

perceives mockery
in the disparity
between its chipped, rusted edges
and dawn's smooth horizon

and with malicious glee
slashes madly—
carving blue skies
good health
a tenuous inner peace
into confetti

## The Juggler And The Alley Cat

as I lie barely awake
in the morning half-light
I see something I hadn't seen before—
beauty in the chaos of her life

I have a vision of her
entering a room in her usual rush
from one job or appointment
to another
and how she lays waste to it
like a caffeinated hurricane

scattering clothes
shoes and tote bags
paperwork and bills
and coffee cups everywhere
cabinet doors bang
dishes clatter

she talks to a client
on the phone
while tapping at the keyboard
and taking small bites
of her sandwich

then she's out the door
again, "ciao babe!"

it's breathtaking
like watching a circus performer
ride a unicycle
across a tightrope
while juggling fire

I feel small
beside her embrace
of the way things are
her ability
to remain human
and smile
and even laugh
in the midst of chaos

I wish I could do that
but I go through life
with all the grace
of an alley cat
being shoved into a sack

so all her plans
and half-finished projects
become objects of ridicule

and because there's still a wound
some words she spoke—
true words

about me
and my angry alley cat ways

I can never let her know
of my admiration
I can only write about it

maybe I'll leave this for her
when I finally go someday

tack it to the fridge
like a suicide note

## The View From Here

this is just to say
I'm in awe of people
who know what they want

she wanted to be a doctor
from the time
she was a little girl

or he wanted to be a cop
just like his old man

and they made it happen
and they smile more often
than others

I guess when you know
you know
and the path is defined

you don't spend your life
stumbling around
through the brush
towards one false summit
after another

but...hell—
the view from here
is pretty spectacular too
and it's mine

## NIGHT AT MY THROAT

there's no flags or cairns
anywhere in sight

## Told You

I sometimes still
hold out my hand
to those who laugh
like hyenas
who smile like wolves
with bloody canines

and then draw back
a stump
shocked, but smiling
as I mock the mirror me
and say "I told you...."

## Too Late

I see the photo—
a friend, his beautiful wife
on vacation...someplace tropical
a cheek to cheek selfie in a hammock
colorful cocktails with fruit and little umbrellas
"Love my wife...and my life."
reads the caption
I should be happy, but...
as I stare at it
I hear the rusted gears
I hear rats teeth at the bone
I hear my gut groan with the undigested
and quickly scroll—
get this off my screen
and out of my world
but it's too late—
their happiness elbows my ribs
I limp back to it
tap the heart, send the love that
costs me nothing (but does it?)
then I flick the image
from the glass—like snot
and try to sleep through the cacophony
of my solitary breath
soft against the pillow

## Transference

As I chatted with a friend
about my recent trip to the sea,
and about his years spent
working the fishing boats,
it suddenly occurred to me:
that as many hours
as I've pleasantly wasted
gazing over her varied surface,
and listening to her music,
and even venturing in,
to swim a little,
to ride the waves,
to feel the currents
and the undertow as she tries
to draw me in deeper—

I do not really know her.
She remains a stranger to me,
a mystery.

Maybe if I knew her as he does,
("That vicious bitch!")
I wouldn't feel about her, the way I do.
And isn't that always the way?

Maybe "known" and "loved"
are opposites,
despite the old song.

# NIGHT AT MY THROAT

So I keep my distance,
my delusions,
and my love
alive.

## Twist Of Grain

On my snowshoes I crunch
over an icy crust from clump
to clump of dwarf evergreens,
seeking shelter from wind blown
wraiths.  I find a spot, and huddle
here awhile, Tahoe blue below,
Mount Rose at my back.

As I sit on this rock wondering
just how far I'd have to go,
to escape what I've dragged
up here with me, what I seem
to drag everywhere without end,
I see it—beyond this last stand
of crooked pines, a lone tree
protruding from the snow.  Two
feet high, and already bent like a
U-turn away from the sunlight.
It'll never grow straight, but it'll grow.
You could transplant it, maybe.
Carry it down the mountain,
place it in rich, dark soil and
bind it to stakes, direct its path.

But the tension, the memory
within that twist of grain
would always tug at the rope,
wanting to bend.  In a mere
tree, we don't call this will,

or choice. That's a privilege
reserved for ourselves—
lucky sons of bitches we are.

# Want

I don't want to sit here
painfully sober and aware
counting my breaths
feeling the feelings
the flickering flame of karma
as it burns me up

I want a cold six pack
I want a bottle
I want to get a hotel room
and a pile of blow
and try to break my record
of three hookers in the same day

or maybe fall for someone
20 years younger
and make a goddamn fool
of myself

the world will see us
and laugh
and I won't give a shit
because they just don't get it

and then
when it's over
when I'm used up
and she's moved on
to the next

## NIGHT AT MY THROAT

I want to self-destruct
dramatically
spectacularly
like you see
on the big screen

hell....maybe they'll even
make a movie about it
from my point of view

it ends with the rushing of air
the pavement coming fast
then a sick crunch
and a cut to black

## What We Give

Our bitter bile, our darkest
spleen, our venom. Our
swollen livers, track marks,
prison tattoos. Our chaos,
our madness, our suicide
attempts. The ashes of our fig
leaves, wrapped in red bows.

We stand naked, our wounds
exposed. Jagged and mutinous
lips, hastily sewn. They must
speak…or die, and us with them.
They open, tear stitches, spill
stories like blood. A transfusion.

We search your eyes—
something…anything but
the cold stare, the judgement
we're used to. The true desire
is folded, tucked away—
the mirage of a mother's
face, the expression she wears,
kissing a skinned knee.

We seek with a deluded hope
that later turns on us—
like a lion who tries, time and
again, to lay down with the
lamb, but finally gives up,
devours him, and is filled.

## Whispers

it's the whispers
that are really worse
and more subtly vicious
in the long run

our old tapes run in the background
staticky and overplayed
soft echoes of ridicule
of shame and fear

we float in this sound
like an ocean of amniotic fluid

we're swaddled
by layers of messages
like warm blankets
like straitjackets

there's a homeless guy
who wanders into the coffee shop sometimes
early in the morning
he sits in the corner
whispering, mumbling

if he started screaming
they'd throw him out, but no—
he just mutters softly to himself

as I ignore him with one ear
and listen with the other

some days I put ear plugs in
that takes care of him
at least

## Wholeness

this modern
(or postmodern)
digital, uploaded
kind of life
feels much
like I imagine death will be
whether I'm buried or burned
whether I'm scattered
by worms or flames
I'll be every bit as disintegrated
as I am now
walking around inside my skin...
my skin—
which provides an appearance
of wholeness
much like a garbage bag

## The Night At My Throat

I did this to myself
with that three-hour nap
this afternoon
and now the night
is at my throat

go...go somewhere
drive out into the desert
to a blacker sky
where the stars
seem too bright

or head downtown
roam the streets
because out there
swathed in neon
is something better
than here

meanwhile I pace
the quiet of the house
as it gnaws at me
like rats chewing
at the walls

I step outside
and gaze
at a few
dim
stars

# THE GRASS THAT COVERS US

## Fatherhood

I am father to none
but this motley tribe of orphans
wandering lonely
through my tangled forests

I cannot help you
my children
but know that I see you
and bear witness
to your struggles

your pain
your lack of fulfillment
your incredible
insatiable longing
is mine too

I witness your search
and your battles
your infighting
the treachery
the duplicity

I watch you create gods
for yourselves
then slay them
when they inevitably disappoint
(gods are only human...)

I marvel at your tenacity
as you traverse this wilderness
along old paths
or hack new ones
through weeds grown
tough as iron

seeking a home
yet each step
is within the threshold

## Asking The Question

I couldn't have told you, then
what it was...
what it was that drew me
to all of you

you might just as well
have asked a newborn
his first impression
of the outside world

I can only guess at it now
who, or what it was I sought
in your sundry eyes and guises

what flame
what shadow
what part of this dance
escapes our understanding?

we ask the question many ways
clutching the long tresses of the void
with thoughts and words
with eyes and fingertips
with ears, lips, and tongue
with every footstep, breath, and heartbeat
until we're planted back in the ground

and after—
the grass that covers us

will ask the wind
and the wind will answer
with a hiss

## How It Might Be

if you want to know
how it might be for us someday
pay attention to the little ones
as the nights grow cold

watch the moth stumble in the grass
you can hold him in your hand
toss him to the wind
but he won't fly again

see the flies buzz in through every crack
only to perish on window sills
their scattered hollow shells
don't deter the others

observe the viciousness of bees
as the flowers wither
how they harass and swarm
when you roll the cans out on trash day

notice how the mice
chew everything in sight
how the previously inedible
now becomes appetizing

witness how they race boldly
across the kitchen floor
crossing our giant shadows
risking everything, for a crumb

## To Dig, Pace, And Chew

it's not the lack of answers
that dig the hole
but the asking of questions
each one another shovelful
until you hit the bedrock of the final one—
then wear the stone smooth
beneath your pacing soles
as you stare upwards
at a grave shaped space of sky
beyond walls of crumbling dirt
wondering if what's left—
this lonely and unhappy life
a life that's far too often
like a wad of gum drained
of its flavor and sweetness—
is still worth chewing

## Understandable

the clouds are nebulas today
but they do not collapse
and burst into stars
or darken to storms and rain

they spread sheer white wings
they cover the sky
like torn stockings tossed to the wind
hints of blue beauty beneath

an understandable flight—
to drift and scatter
into an emptiness nearly pure
to be everywhere all at once

## Stray

maybe it's autumn
the cold nights
how dead leaves scratch
down the alleyway
like this stray at my door
the same one I've driven off
many times in a rage

but tonight
I'm tired of fighting
so I let him in
he shivers
wet from the rain
holds no grudges
as he huddles beside me
as we sit and listen
to sad songs together
songs now old
and allow ourselves
to remember

# TWO POEMS

## Worms

A mother sits her ten year old
daughter down over lattes and tells
her in an earnest tone how disappointed
she is at her choice of clothing.
She pinches a fold of the girl's baggy
sweatshirt between a thumb and forefinger
like body fat calipers, and with a face that
just sucked a lemon, says "tomorrow
I want you to wear the shirt we just
bought, with that vest, and I want
the vest zipped up, and if I need to I can
call your teacher to make sure…"

After, mom gets up to use the bathroom,
leaving the girl alone, staring into her cup.
She raises her eyes and sees me, but before I
can give her the smile I so desperately want to
give her, she looks away again. Stares at the
table as the words burrow, doing their job—
the way worms soften soil for a thousand
seeds, cast by careless hands or shifting
winds. I swear I can even hear them.
From ten feet away. I can hear their
horrible tiny mouths chewing, gnawing,
tunneling deep inside her.

## Disciple

like having my ear
to a bowl of Rice Krispies...
but with the snaps, crackles and pops
occurring less frequently

puzzled, I wander the yard
searching for the source—
a warm day...sunshine...
pinecones!
on the tree...opening

yet another thing
previously unnoticed
now I know
and smile at knowing

how I wish
more discoveries
were like that

and if the cones are opening
from simple sunlight
and warmth...
then maybe I'll just sit here
all day

# YELLOW BIRD

## A Little Longer

Often as I walk the headland paths
I will happen upon a lonely beach somewhere
in a little cove
with a stream trickling down
beneath piles of bleached driftwood logs
like scattered dinosaur bones
resting on a bed of pebbles
broken shells
and other shattered
and unrecognizable things
coughed up by the ocean
and left there for us to ponder

I like to sit amid all that brokenness
that tangled mass of life and death
to walk around and feel at home in it
to pick through piles of seashells
with edges sharp as broken beer bottles
sifting the chaos
searching just to search
a little longer

## Thank You, Sir

It's the tone, he said.
Poetry that's suited
to a barroom lectern.
It rants and rambles.
My god, but I have heard
the most marvelous
rambling rants from
barroom lecterns, from
miserable, drunken bastards—
much better than most
poetry I've ever read,
with more honesty,
guts and heart, and
closer to god, even.
Shit…O'Neill wrote a
couple of great plays about
miserable, drunken bastards,
whose rambling finally
circled around and stumbled
right into the truth, as
rambling often does.
So thank you, sir.
Sincerely, thank you.

## No Matter What You Say

the tiniest yellow bird
perches in the sycamore

it sings a beautiful song
a varied and indescribable song

a song I've never heard
it sings for me

it sings for me...yes—
no matter what you say

there have been mornings
I might have yelled—

what the hell have you got
to sing about?

but this is not one of them
this is not one of them, and

I think I'd like to come back
as that—as the tiniest

yellow bird, who sings
to the people going into work

who'll sing to the people
who will work in these buildings

when I'm gone
who'll sing a beautiful

and varied and indescribable song
to their frantic and worried souls

who'll sing to them…even
if they curse or throw stones

to come back and sing like that—
yes…I think I will

## *Acknowledgements*

The poem "Night At My Throat" first appeared in *Ordinary Trauma*, published in 2019 by Alien Buddha Press. Brian Rihlmann has also published widely in online zines and journals including places like *Bold Monkey, The Pike Press, Yellow Mama, As It Ought To Be, Hobo Camp Review and Winedrunk Sidewalk, The Song Is, Constellate Magazine, Poppy Road Review, Cajun Mutt Press* and the *Rye Whiskey Review*, to name a few.

## *About The Author*

Brian Rihlmann comes out of a tradition that seems to be fading in our country, that of the self-taught poet. His experiences in jobs as varied as car washes, horse stables, construction and warehousing to bartending, truck driving, working as a personal trainer and commercial photographer, just to name a few, have shaped his work and provided an inexhaustible source of material. His broad work experiences and wide travels in the United States have made him an authentic observer of American values and life. He writes with conviction about racism, the glorification of money, the disrespect for the elderly and the poor, and about the American gun culture. He is currently sheltering in place near Reno, Nevada. He is the author of a previous collection of poems called *Ordinary Trauma* and is widely published online.

CPSIA information can be obtained
at www.ICGtesting.com
Printed in the USA
BVHW031814010421
603948BV00015B/77